stay grounded

stay grounded

A guided journal for times of change, upheaval, or stress

KRISTINE PIDKAMENY

CICO BOOKS
LONDON NEW YORK

Published in 2021 by CICO Books
An imprint of Ryland Peters & Small Ltd
20–21 Jockey's Fields   341 E 116th St
London WC1R 4BW   New York, NY 10029

www.rylandpeters.com

10 9 8 7 6 5 4 3 2 1

A CIP catalog record for this book is available from the Library
of Congress and the British Library.

Flexiback ISBN: 978-1-80065-035-0
Paperback ISBN: 978-1-80065-051-0

Printed in China

Senior editor: Carmel Edmonds
Senior designer: Emily Breen
Art director: Sally Powell
Production manager: Gordana Simakovic
Publishing manager: Penny Craig
Publisher: Cindy Richards

contents

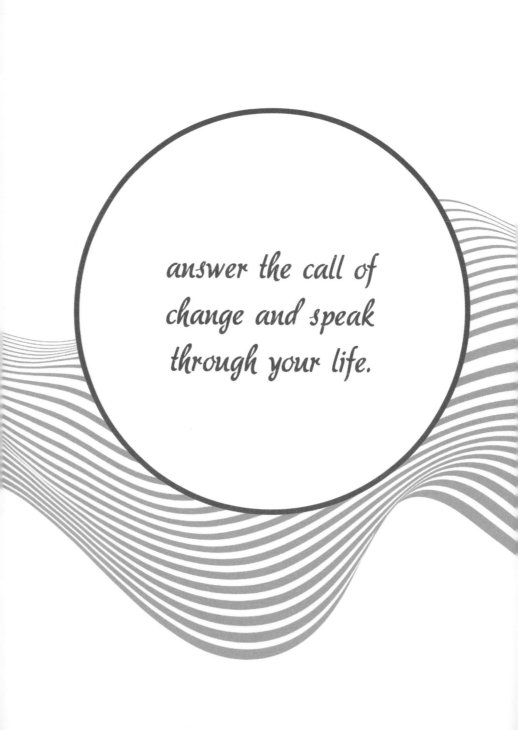

answer the call of change and speak through your life.

introduction

Change is a constant in life, but when it's the unfavorable sort, finding a stable place to land can feel out of reach. It's easy to feel overwhelmed when faced with unsettling circumstances. It's also a natural first reaction. However, how you engage with the changes and those feelings is key to feeling more centered. Uncertainty and stress are inevitable parts of life. Spending time with yourself, becoming more aware of what's going on in your head and heart, and reflecting upon your daily life and activities will all help you to stay grounded.

This guided journal offers a place of support, exploration, and inspiration. It is filled with interactive prompts, meditations, and the space to write freely to help you process your emotions and consider options and solutions. Just the simple act of writing your thoughts and feelings down on paper can bring about a sense of relief during times of change. It helps you see how things really are, and the next step is not resisting them. As you move beyond the internal chatter that gets stirred up during times of uncertainty, you gain greater perspective. Discovering there are things you can control and things that you cannot invites clarity and insight. Knowing the difference between them and taking responsibility for the things you can change helps you get your footing again. Reflecting on all you've gotten through and finding the silver linings allow you to step forward with courage.

how to use this journal

The chapters are designed to be completed in order, as each section builds upon the previous one. Of course, if a particular area calls out to you more than another on a particular day, go for it. You are your trusted companion on this journey.

CHAPTER 1 *start where you are*

Begin with the power of acceptance. Simply being in the present moment, even when it's uncomfortable, is vital for what comes next. By setting the stage, you are making room to listen to your needs and wants.

CHAPTER 2 *who, what, where, and when*

Take a closer look at your attitudes and actions to gain a better understanding of yourself. Consider your thoughts, conversations, and behaviors. Are they critical or reassuring? Mean-spirited or kind? Dismissive or valuing? Which attitudes would be more useful for your wellbeing? It is possible to change to a more self-compassionate approach.

CHAPTER 3 *mindful moments*

Cultivate time to pay attention to both your inner and outer life. Learning to pause and breathe during a demanding experience is one way to help you reassess what's going on and refocus on the situation. Discover a variety of ways to reconnect with what your mind, body, and heart are saying to you and find more peace and calm.

CHAPTER 4 *giving thanks*

Gratitude is a universal reminder of many things, including the beauty, hope, and joy in life. You can choose to express and practice appreciation, of both yourself and others. In doing so, you will feel more centered and empowered, which helps in better managing stress.

CHAPTER 5 *quiet strength*

Worry, fear, and anxiety do not define you. Explore difficulties and disappointments further—what are they asking of you? Get curious to see if the answer is hidden in the question. Sometimes things break down in order to break through: it could be the pieces are actually falling together, rather than falling apart.

CHAPTER 6 *the time is now*

Set the tone for your day and welcome a rich and full life. You have the potential to increase your capacity to adapt to the changes in life and find more balance. Maybe you can even learn to celebrate the unexpected. Having a vision that things can be better is a reminder that you can put a plan in place and make it happen.

choose to be unstoppable.

journaling suggestions

If you are new to journaling, or even if you're a regular writer, the following tips may be helpful.

- Continuity is important, so show up even when you'd rather not.
- Establish a writing routine in a space that works best for you.
- Create a personal ritual to mark this special time of exploration.
- Take time to pause with self-compassion, especially when feeling tired, stuck, or frustrated.
- Remain grateful for your words and the places they guide you to.
- Remember what brings you joy and comfort.
- Follow your own lead.

there is only one you

In an ever-changing world of highs, lows, and everything in between, the twists and turns of your journey are unique to your life. While it's true at certain times we all face similar questions in dealing with change and adversity, and may handle them in similar ways, there's no perfect one-size-fits-all solution. Different approaches work for different people and how things turn out can be quite individual.

How you respond to what happens in life is a choice—your choice. It's freeing to know that when difficult situations arise, you can decide how you will meet them. Learning how to stay grounded is an essential skill in a life well lived. Let your instincts guide you and you'll find your way—the one that works best for you.

*the power is
in your hands.*

CHAPTER 1

start where you are

Welcome the unfolding present

Feeling at home or in tune with your body is a benefit of being grounded. When you feel ungrounded it can adversely affect your life, including emotions, relationships, focus, and sleep patterns. A simple way to ground yourself is to start with your body first, tapping into your senses and the present environment.

Settle into the present moment and describe the details of your surroundings.

Did you consciously choose this location to write in your journal? Why?

Describe in detail what you are wearing now.

Are you comfortable or uncomfortable in your clothing?
Are these favorite or unfavorite choices, and why?

Sitting with both feet on the ground, take a moment and notice the contact your body has with where you are sitting. Focus your attention, beginning with your feet and moving up through your body, and describe those different areas.

How did you feel before and after the above experience?

Close your eyes and take five easy breaths. For a few moments, tune into your senses and pay attention to the sounds and scents around you, the temperature against your skin, and any internal images that may arise within. What did you experience?

_____

_____

_____

_____

_____

_____

_____

_____

_____

Now, with your eyes open, scan your present environment and pick something that especially stands out to you. Describe what you see and why you made this choice.

_____

_____

_____

_____

_____

_____

_____

_____

_____

_____

_____

Acceptance is about getting more familiar with feeling comfortable when uncomfortable. It's the caring reminder that it's okay to not feel okay—and also to know you are fine as you are.

How are you feeling in this moment? Is there a particular situation, person, or experience that influences your feelings now?

_____

_____

_____

_____

_____

_____

_____

_____

_____

_____

_____

_____

_____

_____

_____

_____

_____

_____

_____

_____

_____

_____

Be still for a few moments with your eyes closed. Follow your breath. Name the thoughts you notice running through your mind.

_____

_____

_____

_____

_____

_____

_____

_____

_____

_____

What is your experience after putting these thoughts to pen and paper?

_____

_____

_____

_____

_____

_____

_____

_____

_____

_____

_____

_____

_____

_____

Stand up from where you are sitting. Walk about for five minutes and get some movement going in your body—maybe shaking your hands a bit, shrugging your shoulders up and down, or making different facial expressions—whatever feels right for you at the moment. You can even vary it up. Describe your movements and how you felt afterwards.

Lie face up on the floor, or on the ground if you are writing outdoors. Take a few moments and notice the different points of contact your body has beneath you. What are they and how do they feel?

_____

_____

_____

_____

_____

_____

_____

_____

_____

_____

Now take a few moments to focus on the surrounding space above your body and how it feels. Describe your experience and any different sensations from the previous practice.

_____

_____

_____

_____

_____

_____

_____

_____

_____

_____

_____

Make a list of the words you associate with feeling "ungrounded" and next to each word a situation that relates to it.

_____   _____
_____   _____
_____   _____
_____   _____
_____   _____
_____   _____
_____   _____
_____   _____
_____   _____
_____   _____
_____   _____

Make a list of the words you associate with feeling "grounded" and next to each word an activity that relates to it.

_____   _____
_____   _____
_____   _____
_____   _____
_____   _____
_____   _____
_____   _____
_____   _____
_____   _____
_____   _____

Imagine your feelings of ungrounded and grounded have just met and are being introduced to one another. Write a few lines of dialogue from their first conversation.

be yourself: everyone else is taken.

Resisting change often brings on more suffering to an already difficult situation. Consider that your anxiety or feeling of being overwhelmed in response to your challenges could be a positive call to wake up to a better way for yourself.

Describe a situation that requires a change in your life that you are stressed about and the feelings it brings up.

Imagine that the experience on the opposite page is happening to your best friend and they've come to you for guidance. In what ways can you help them reframe their situation from an obstacle to avoid to an opportunity to take advantage of?

Choose a favorable idea from the above that you can apply to your situation. Create a personal statement from that suggestion to serve as a positive reminder.

Using various shapes, lines, forms, textures, and/or colors, create a collage that expresses how you are feeling now.

What is the title of your collage and why?

_____

_____

_____

_____

_____

_____

_____

_____

_____

_____

_____

_____

Write a few lines to accompany your collage. You could even write a short poem.

_____

_____

_____

_____

_____

_____

_____

_____

_____

_____

_____

_____

_____

Daily rituals and routine have a grounding influence during times of change. Ways to get your feet back on terra firma, either literally or figuratively, include:

- Walking or running outdoors.
- Walking around your living space, taking in your environment.
- Standing still, closing your eyes, and listening.
- Sitting down with your morning drink and simply enjoying drinking it, rather than multitasking.

Decide on a morning ritual you can easily begin each day with, one that you enjoy and encourages wellbeing. Practice consistently for one week and keep track of before and after insights here.

all the flowers
of all the tomorrows
are in the seeds
of today.

Indian proverb

CHAPTER 2

who, what, where, and when

Examine personal beliefs and habits to see how they're working for you

The simple act of writing your thoughts and feelings down on paper can ease emotions and bring balance into your brain. Experiences seem a bit less overwhelming. You can see more clearly and look at what's working for you and what isn't. A sense of relief emerges and the tight grip of anxiety begins to loosen.

Describe a recent stressful experience. Detail the feelings that came up for you in the situation.

Reflect on the experience you described on the opposite page and look at it through new eyes. What might this experience be telling you about yourself? What can you learn from it?

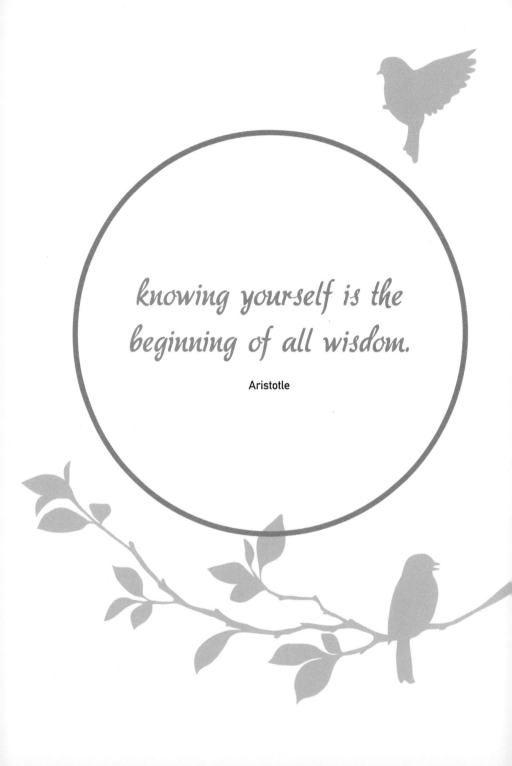

knowing yourself is the
beginning of all wisdom.

Aristotle

What are you most proud about in your life and why?

What do you appreciate most about others in your life and why?

When do you find yourself having disregard for yourself? In what ways?

How might you choose a more self-compassionate approach to the above, rather than judging, ignoring, or making others responsible for those feelings?

Do you prefer attention on yourself or others? In what ways?

Describe a recent situation that relates to the above and how well
that worked out for you.

Who inspires you in your personal circle and why?

_____

_____

_____

_____

_____

_____

_____

_____

_____

_____

_____

Who from history, literature, or the world of celebrity inspires you and why?

_____

_____

_____

_____

_____

_____

_____

_____

_____

_____

_____

_____

_____

Create a list of words and activities that capture a sense of adventure
and imagination for you.

_____

_____

_____

_____

_____

_____

_____

_____

_____

_____

_____

Do you include any of the above in your present life and in what ways?
If not, how might you incorporate them into your life?

_____

_____

_____

_____

_____

_____

_____

_____

_____

_____

_____

_____

_____

Self-care often gets lost in the shuffle at times of unrest. Creating healthy relationships with food, exercise, and your daily routines will benefit you and support you in feeling more grounded.

Describe your typical morning routine, including how you feel upon waking up.

_____

_____

_____

_____

_____

_____

_____

_____

_____

How is this working for you? If you could improve upon it, list a few ideas here.

_____

_____

_____

_____

_____

_____

_____

_____

_____

_____

_____

_____

Describe your typical evening routine, including what you do right before going to sleep.

How is this working for you? If you could improve upon it, list a few ideas here.

When under stress, what foods do you tend to eat or find comforting? Do you eat more or less than you usually do? Does your mealtime schedule change—and if so, how?

_____

_____

_____

_____

_____

_____

_____

_____

_____

Describe the effect of the above. Is it helpful or not? Are there any adjustments, even the slightest one, you can make now for a healthier outcome?

_____

_____

_____

_____

_____

_____

_____

_____

_____

_____

When there's less stress in your life, describe your typical meal preferences
and the times you eat.

_____

_____

_____

_____

_____

_____

_____

_____

_____

_____

_____

Are your above choices beneficial to your wellbeing? If so, choose one
or more you can keep in mind to practice during stressful times.

_____

_____

_____

_____

_____

_____

_____

_____

_____

_____

_____

_____

_____

What are your favorite forms of exercise or movement, and how often are they part of your day? Do you prefer group exercise or to go solo?

_____

_____

_____

_____

_____

_____

_____

_____

_____

_____

What other types of exercise or movement are you curious about? Could you include them in your day? Make a list here and choose one from that list to investigate.

_____

_____

_____

_____

_____

_____

_____

_____

_____

_____

_____

Daily exercise routines and movements often need to be put on hold temporarily during distressful periods, yet these are the times when even the smallest physical effort will make a big difference in keeping you grounded. If only a 5-minute walk is possible, do it. Being consistent helps too. Create your list of modified activities here.

stumbling blocks are simply stepping stones in disguise.

Facing change and a need to balance priorities are constants in life. Fear and confusion may arise while navigating new or challenging situations. Equanimity can help: it means "an even mind" and is a state of being calm and composed. Consider how equanimity might transform stressors to improve upon the outcome, whether within yourself or with others.

How do you typically manage overwhelming worry?

What is your approach to disagreements and disappointments?

Describe a recent situation that worried you to no end and its impact on other areas of your life.

_____
_____
_____
_____
_____
_____
_____
_____
_____
_____
_____

Have your ways of handling the emotions and situations described in the previous three prompts been effective? If not, what steps can you take to improve upon them?

_____
_____
_____
_____
_____
_____
_____
_____
_____
_____
_____
_____

What are your favorite ways to relax? Include any hobbies or activities you enjoy. How often do you include them in your day?

_____
_____
_____
_____
_____
_____
_____
_____
_____
_____

Create a list of ways to find downtime, no matter how minimal, to maintain balance during stressful periods.

_____
_____
_____
_____
_____
_____
_____
_____
_____
_____
_____

Which people and/or community groups do you turn to for support
during difficult times?

_____

_____

_____

_____

_____

_____

_____

_____

_____

_____

_____

_____

In what ways does your connection with the above help you? Do you need
to expand your circle of support? If so, how might you do this?

_____

_____

_____

_____

_____

_____

_____

_____

_____

_____

_____

_____

_____

_____

Describe the details of where you live now—the location, general home environment, and if you share your space with other people or pets.

_____

_____

_____

_____

_____

_____

_____

_____

_____

_____

How satisfied are you with your current living situation? Does it provide the comfort and room you need, especially during unsettling times?

_____

_____

_____

_____

_____

_____

_____

_____

_____

_____

_____

_____

Describe some ways to enhance your environment for more wellbeing
and enjoyment now.

_____

_____

_____

_____

_____

_____

_____

_____

_____

_____

_____

Make a list of longer-term changes to your living situation so that you can
plan to make them when the time is right.

_____

_____

_____

_____

_____

_____

_____

_____

_____

_____

_____

_____

_____

Financial security contributes to your sense of stability. Describe the current state of your personal finances. Be truthful—this journal is for your eyes only.

_____
_____
_____
_____
_____
_____
_____
_____
_____

Are there any areas of concern in need of improvement? If so, brainstorm possible solutions.

_____
_____
_____
_____
_____
_____
_____
_____
_____
_____
_____
_____

Make a list of what you value in life.

Reflect on the above list. Consider which things originated from you and truly matter to you, and which have been influenced by others in order to meet their expectations of you.

During times of uncertainty, what is the storyline you typically tell yourself? Do you consider yourself to be surviving or thriving? For either scenario, write about a recent situation and how you felt afterwards.

Reflect on how you feel about your values, beliefs, and way of living now.

know the value of
knowing your value.

CHAPTER 3

mindful moments

Increase awareness and find calm through
basic mindfulness practices

You can take the edge off stress during uncertain, worrisome times. Through mindful awareness, such as paying attention to your breath, you welcome a sense of calm presence and feeling more grounded.

When feeling worried or under stress today, take time to notice your breathing. Describe the situation or thoughts that have stirred up these uneasy feelings and the quality and pattern of your breathing.

Pause and take a moment to focus on your breathing. Close your eyes. Inhale through your nose for 4 counts. Exhale for 4 counts, or longer if you can, preferably through your nose. Keep your breath moving slowly and gently. Repeat 5 times. Describe how you felt after this practice.

make space for your breath and be calm today.

Becoming more aware of your physical body and movements is helpful for feeling grounded.

Start with your hands as you write here. Describe the position of your writing hand (your dominant hand) and how it feels as you write.

_____

_____

_____

_____

_____

_____

_____

_____

What is your other hand (your non-dominant hand) doing now?
How is it positioned and how does it feel?

_____

_____

_____

_____

_____

_____

_____

_____

_____

_____

Take a moment and write a couple of sentences using your non-dominant hand. How does this feel?

Consider the space between your two hands (dominant and non-dominant) as you write. Outline a brief conversation between your dominant and non-dominant hand and what goes on in that space between the two.

Describe the posture of your body as you write here. Are you comfortable or uncomfortable? Do you stay still while writing or are you more inclined to move position as you write?

What is the story your body is telling you now?

Thoughts and actions can become scattered during times of change or upheaval. You may feel numb or disconnected, like you are spreading your life too thin. Bringing your awareness to your center within helps you gain focus and connection, making you feel whole again.

Recount a recent experience when there was too much going on and you found your thoughts, actions, and feelings were out of sync with each other.

Set a timer for five minutes. Get comfortable sitting up with your back straight and both feet on the floor. Breathe easily and focus on your solar plexus, a point located above your navel and below your sternum. Imagine this point is a golden yellow sun bathing you in self-confidence. Inhale and exhale the sun's energy flowing into your center and out from your center. Reflect on how you felt before and after this practice.

a garden is a delight
to the eye and a solace
for the soul.

Saadi

Tuning into each of your senses—sight, sound, touch, smell, taste—in the here and now is a simple and effective way to invite present moment awareness. You can do this anywhere at any time.

With eyes open, slowly scan your surroundings. Choose one item to focus on and spend a few minutes paying close attention to what you notice, such as texture, color, and shape. Describe what you see in detail here.

Pick a time today or this week and try the above practice outdoors.
Describe your experience.

Close your eyes and spend a few minutes listening to the sounds of your surroundings. Describe what you hear.

Is there a particular sound that stands out from others? What makes it distinctive? Notice how it makes you feel. Write about your experience here.

Pick a time today or this week to immerse yourself in nature sounds, either outdoors or on a soundtrack. You can also do this with a favorite piece of instrumental music or song. Focus on one detail that catches your attention—perhaps the rhythm, an instrument, or a word or phrase. Describe your experience.

Become more aware of your sense of touch and explore your immediate environment—for example, the feel of your writing implement, the surface area and paper of this journal, the fabric of your clothing, or the texture of your hair. Describe your experience.

For one week, choose a different activity each day to tap into your sense of touch—perhaps walking barefoot, washing dishes, petting an animal, folding laundry, or holding a special stone or keepsake in your hand. Explore both indoor and outdoor settings. Describe your experiences here.

Monday

Tuesday

Wednesday

Thursday

Friday

Saturday

Sunday

With eyes closed, take a moment to place your attention on the smells of your present surroundings. Pungent or mild? Pleasing or not? Any memories stirred? Describe your experience.

_____

_____

_____

_____

_____

_____

_____

_____

_____

Take a walk outside, pausing for a moment to be still. Close your eyes and practice the above. Write about your experience.

_____

_____

_____

_____

_____

_____

_____

_____

_____

Explore the world of aromatherapy and the self-care benefits for relaxation and grounding. There are various essential oils to choose from and simple ways to incorporate them into your lifestyle. For example, lavender encourages relaxation and can be easily used with a diffuser, in bath salts, or with a scented candle.

List a few ways you can include aromatherapy in your home, while you work and/or while meditating. Experiment and see what suits you best.

Savor a mindful moment with your sense of taste. Take a fruit you can peel easily, such as an orange or banana. Slowly remove the skin from the fruit. Section or cut the fruit into bite-size pieces and arrange them in a pleasing pattern on a plate. Taking your time, select each piece with care and chew slowly. Focus on the taste, texture, and temperature. Describe your experience and how you felt before and afterwards.

Decide on a mealtime this week when you can eat slowly and only pay attention to eating. Focus on one item from your meal. Imagine you are a professional taste tester and must evaluate and describe the flavor of this one item in detail.

_____

_____

_____

_____

_____

_____

_____

_____

_____

_____

_____

Continue eating the rest of your meal slowly. If you wish, follow the above practice with other parts of the meal. Describe your overall taste experience and how it differs from your usual meals.

_____

_____

_____

_____

_____

_____

_____

_____

_____

_____

_____

_____

Words are powerful tools for healing, uplifting, and improving your life. Whether through the words you think, read, speak, or listen to, a mindful approach can have a transformative effect on your greater wellbeing.

Take time today to pay close attention to the words and phrases you use in conversation with others and/or in your own thoughts. List a few examples and the effect they have on you.

Observe the words you are exposed to in your outer world today, such as from others, in reading, or what you take in from the news or on social media. List a few examples and the effect they have on you.

Note any words or phrases from the previous two prompts you can reframe for a more beneficial impact on your wellbeing.

Energy flows where attention goes. The repetition of certain words or mantras can have a positive influence to quiet your mind and reduce racing or wandering thoughts.

Create a list of calming words you can repeat to yourself to settle your mind during times of anxiety—for example, ease, serenity, and calm. Words that evoke a tranquil environment or memory for you will be helpful, too.

Create a list of personal mantras or phrases that you can repeat
to yourself or keep posted nearby as calming reminders.

*I choose peace
over this.*

CHAPTER 4

giving thanks

Consider all you can be grateful for

Gratitude is a choice. Expressing and practicing gratitude is beneficial for feeling centered and empowered through both easy and difficult times. The good experiences are richer and the hard ones more bearable. Choosing to refocus your attention and make room for appreciation during tough moments helps reduce the effects of stress.

In your daily routine, what are you most grateful for and why? Be specific.

Describe in detail three qualities you appreciate most about yourself and why.

1

2

3

Describe in detail three qualities you appreciate most in other people and why.

1

2

3

Modern conveniences vary and are relative to location and lifestyle, such as getting clean drinking water from a tap or having a faster online connection. Name five that improve and make your life easier.

1 _____

2 _____

3 _____

4 _____

5 _____

List five people you are grateful for and specifically why. Include both people you are close to, such as family and friends, and others you don't know as well though perhaps see often in your community, such as a delivery person or medical professional.

1 _____

2 _____

3 _____

4 _____

5 _____

Choose a person you are close to from your list on the previous page and express your gratitude to them in words or through an action. Describe your experience.

_____

_____

_____

_____

_____

_____

_____

_____

_____

_____

Choose a person you don't know as well from your list on the previous page and express your gratitude to them in words or through an action. Describe your experience.

_____

_____

_____

_____

_____

_____

_____

_____

_____

_____

_____

Write in depth about an uplifting event in your life you are grateful
for and explain why.

Write in depth about a challenging past experience, which in retrospect surprised you with unexpected benefits.

List a few foods from one of your meals today and consider where each item has come from and the people who have been involved in getting it to your table.

_____

_____

_____

_____

_____

_____

_____

_____

_____

Compose a note of thanks in general to all involved in the above process.

_____

_____

_____

_____

_____

_____

_____

_____

_____

_____

_____

_____

Select one room in your home and describe five things in that room you are grateful for and why.

1 _____

2 _____

3 _____

4 _____

5 _____

In the above room you selected, describe an experience you've had there you are grateful for.

_____

_____

_____

_____

_____

_____

_____

_____

_____

_____

_____

_____

Write a letter to yourself and reflect on what your life would be like
without all that you find yourself grateful for now.

Paying it forward means instead of paying someone back for a good deed, you do a good deed for someone else—it creates a ripple of gratitude and good feeling.

List seven ways, no matter how small, that you can pay it forward and inspire gratitude in others. For example, paying for the coffee of the person behind you at the coffee shop, or letting someone in a hurry on a store line go ahead of you.

1

2

3

4

5

6

7

Think about your ancestors who made it possible for you to be here today.
Who are the ones that stand out to you most and why?

_____

_____

_____

_____

_____

_____

_____

_____

_____

Choose one person from your above lineage. If you could speak to them
now, what words of gratitude would you offer to them?

_____

_____

_____

_____

_____

_____

_____

_____

_____

_____

_____

Take a walk outdoors and observe the nature surrounding you.
Recount three things you give thanks for. Be as specific as you can.

1 _____

_____

2 _____

_____

3 _____

_____

Imagine offering your personal message of gratitude to the world
in skywriting. What would it say? Draw your message here.

Each morning for one week, start your day by writing about
one thing you are grateful for.

Monday
_____
_____

Tuesday
_____
_____

Wednesday
_____
_____

Thursday
_____
_____

Friday
_____
_____

Saturday
_____
_____

Sunday
_____
_____

Each evening for one week, write about one thing
you are grateful for from your day.

Monday

Tuesday

Wednesday

Thursday

Friday

Saturday

Sunday

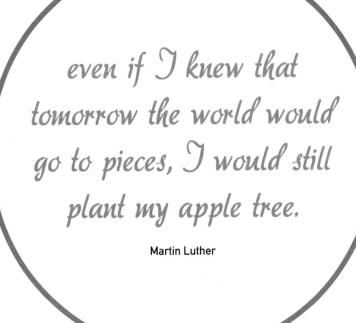

even if I knew that tomorrow the world would go to pieces, I would still plant my apple tree.

Martin Luther

Acknowledge your journey of staying grounded with a symbol of gratitude that is meaningful for you. Perhaps you could plant something you can tend to and watch grow, indoors or outside, or choose a special stone that you keep on hand as a reminder. What is your symbol and why?

Reflect upon your experience with your symbol of gratitude. Do you look at it regularly through the day, or from time to time through the week? How does it make you feel?

CHAPTER 5

quiet strength

Develop greater resilience after setbacks
or upsetting events

Resilience is key to facing life's inevitable challenges. "How to change with change?" is a revealing and informative question to think about, especially after an unfortunate experience. Taking the time to consider a new perspective to see the opportunity in a past difficulty is useful. In choosing a mindset of growth, you will better adapt in the future and feel more grounded in your life.

Describe a recent challenging experience and how you reacted in the situation.

What do your particular reactions on the opposite page reveal to you? For example, sometimes your emotions can quickly get triggered by someone's comments and cloud your response or judgment.

_____

_____

_____

_____

_____

_____

_____

_____

_____

_____

List three positives about the experience you described opposite, no matter how minor they may seem. For example, if you said something you regretted in the situation, this experience is a positive reminder to pause and think more carefully before speaking next time.

1 _____

_____

2 _____

_____

3 _____

_____

Write about a situation you believe you have no control over.

_____
_____
_____
_____
_____
_____
_____
_____
_____
_____

How often do you find yourself dwelling on situations that are out of your control? Describe the feelings that come up.

_____
_____
_____
_____
_____
_____
_____
_____
_____
_____

Name three things you *can* control in your daily life and describe the
feelings that come up from each one.

1 _____

_____

2 _____

_____

3 _____

_____

From the above examples, compose a reminder you can say to yourself
each day, and also revisit when an upsetting event takes place. You may
wish to keep it on hand as a written or digital note.

_____

_____

_____

_____

_____

_____

_____

_____

_____

_____

_____

we never know
how high we are till
we are called to rise;
and then, if we are true
to plan, our statures
touch the skies.

Emily Dickinson

Seeing possibilities and having a vision that things can be better contributes to developing greater resilience. Getting up after a fall is significant. Have empathy and remind yourself you can make this happen. Self-kindness can include:

- Watching your inner critic and giving yourself permission to be imperfect
- Remembering you're not alone and that others share your experience
- Taking time for self-care

In what ways do you practice being kind to yourself after a setback?

List three more ways you can practice self-compassion at these times.

1

2

3

What matters is not what happens to you, it's what you do with it.

Name a first step you can take to center yourself the next time an
upsetting event takes place.

Resolve to put that first step into action. When you do, write about
the outcome here.

Change and adversity will appear in different ways throughout your life, often unexpectedly. Discovering a variety of effective methods that work for you in facing and working through difficulties is valuable.

Explore your flexibility in considering other approaches you might take to stay more grounded. List three different approaches.

1 _____

_____

2 _____

_____

3 _____

_____

Resolve to put one of the above approaches into action. When you do, describe the outcome here.

_____

_____

_____

_____

_____

_____

_____

_____

_____

Write about a recent setback you have had and how you thought about the situation afterwards, and if you still think about it now. Do you get caught up in negative thought patterns, judge yourself harshly, or catastrophize the experience?

_____

_____

_____

_____

_____

_____

_____

_____

_____

Consider three ways you can better manage the above in the future, such as breaking stressful repetitive thoughts with some movement or exercise, or carrying a touchstone to remind yourself of hope rather than worry.

1 _____

_____

2 _____

_____

3 _____

_____

Describe a recent upset and how you talked about the experience
with other people.

_____

_____

_____

_____

_____

_____

_____

_____

_____

_____

_____

Notice the language you chose to describe the event. Did your view support
your ability to be more resilient or did it keep you stuck? How might you
reframe it if need be?

_____

_____

_____

_____

_____

_____

_____

_____

_____

_____

_____

Recall how you faced an unsettling past event and focus on how you got through it.

_____

_____

_____

_____

_____

_____

_____

_____

_____

Create a personal statement based on how you got through the above experience to serve as a reminder to keep perspective in the future.

_____

_____

_____

_____

_____

_____

_____

_____

_____

_____

Describe a current situation that is creating upheaval in your life.
How might you apply what you learned from your experience on
the opposite page to the present one?

_storms don't
last forever._

Discovering stability within yourself creates an inner resource that will be readily available for whatever situation you find yourself in.

Take a moment and recreate your body posture when you are tense and in a stressful situation. You may even exaggerate it a bit. Describe what it looks like and how it feels.

Now get back into your stressful body posture from the opposite page and take a moment to slowly come out of the tension in your body—open up, unfold and stretch your body, notice your feet on the floor, perhaps sit or stand up straighter. Describe what it looks like and how it feels.

_____

_____

_____

_____

_____

_____

_____

_____

_____

Commit to memory how your body feels in the above position and consider accessing this new posture in the future when you need to stay grounded. Keep track here of your experience.

_____

_____

_____

_____

_____

_____

_____

_____

When on shaky ground, in what ways does your sense of stability depend on the outside world and others around you?

_____

_____

_____

_____

_____

_____

_____

_____

_____

_____

What inner resources do you typically access during a time of upset?

_____

_____

_____

_____

_____

_____

_____

_____

_____

_____

_____

_____

A balance of both inner and outer resources to tap into is helpful during difficult times and after them.

Name the people and/or community groups in your life who are sources of support and inspiration for you.

Describe the ways they extend their encouragement to you.

There are rewards after a setback. No longer engaging in a particular struggle provides immediate relief. Facing and moving through each challenge is empowering. Believing in your capacity to cope and discovering new personal strengths along the way develops greater resilience.

Create a list of personal qualities and abilities that you can draw upon in times of adversity.

Create a list of the personal qualities and skills you want to expand upon.

be the type of person you want to meet.

From the center circle below, fill in other words that begin with "g" and that represent inspiration and meaning for you. For example, growth, grace, etc. This is your "grounded" mind map.

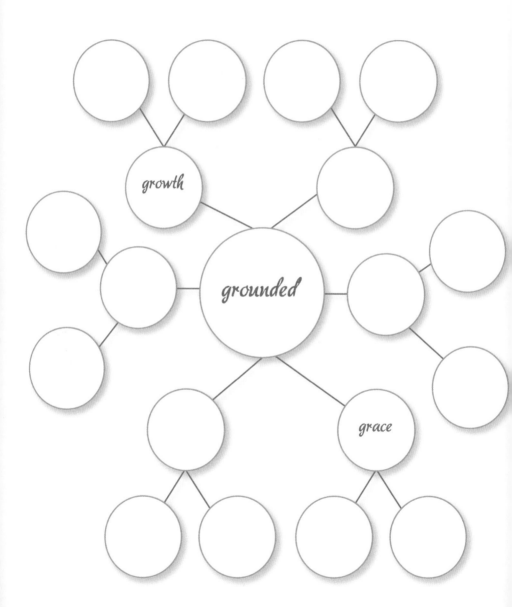

Reflect upon the words from your mind map on the opposite page. Use some of these words to compose a letter to yourself describing what resilience means to you personally in your life now.

CHAPTER 6

the time is now

Focus on positive plans for today
and beyond

Having a constructive plan in place is worthwhile for managing stress when things around you are spiraling out of control. Identifying your priorities and maintaining healthy lifestyle habits will support staying focused and in charge of your choices. You'll also be much less vulnerable to reacting to triggers that have a negative effect on your wellbeing.

Create a lifestyle checklist. Take a look at the different areas of your life and consider the balance of your physical and emotional habits. Include details for each area and note the choices that are working and the ones that need more attention.

Food and beverage choices
_____

_____

Eating and meal times
_____

_____

Exercise and movement
_____

_____

Self-care
_____

_____

Housekeeping
_____

_____

Nature breaks
_____

_____

Meditation and quiet time

Sleep

Socializing

Creativity and hobbies

Digital device usage and online activity

TV, movies, news, and reading

Other areas

When you feel overwhelmed, you may feel stuck or too busy to stay with your well-intended plan. A routine will work when you aim for what's doable within your current circumstances. Decide what you can complete and follow through on easily. This may mean a shorter walk or meditation for the time being. Consistency is key, as it will ingrain the habit.

Review your lifestyle checklist on the previous pages. Choose one area and an associated activity that appeals to you most. Describe the details of the activity here and why it appeals to you.

For one week, carve out 10 minutes each day for the activity you chose on the opposite page. Keep a daily record of how you progress with it and note any reflections and insights at the end of the week.

Day 1

Day 2

Day 3

Day 4

Day 5

Day 6

Day 7

Reflections and insights

Continue with the activity you chose on pages 124–125 for another three weeks. At the end of this time period, give an account of your experience.

_____

_____

_____

_____

_____

_____

_____

_____

_____

Consider if there's another lifestyle area or activity from your checklist you'd like to explore further at present or in the future, as well as or in addition to the previous activity. Keep a list here for reference.

_____

_____

_____

_____

_____

_____

_____

_____

_____

_____

nature does not hurry, yet
everything is accomplished.

Lao Tzu

Daily attention and even the slightest effort to maintain a sense of order is helpful to gain clarity, feel revitalized, and stay grounded.

Look around your living space and identify positive ways to keep order in various areas inside and outside your home:

Kitchen

_____

_____

_____

Bathroom

_____

_____

_____

Bedrooms

_____

_____

_____

Living room

_____

_____

_____

Work space

_____

_____

_____

_____

Hallways/entrances

_____

_____

_____

_____

Basement/attic/storage

_____

_____

_____

_____

Car/garage

_____

_____

_____

_____

Yard/garden/porch

_____

_____

_____

_____

Choose one living area and activity from pages 128–129 you can set in motion each day for one week. Give an account of the outcome.

Build upon your sense of keeping order at home. Choose a different living area and activity from pages 128–129 you can also set in motion each day for one week. Give an account of the outcome.

A worry box or basket can allow you to put aside your anxieties temporarily to give yourself the headspace and mental rest needed to regain perspective and make better decisions. Keep an on-going list here of anything troubling or stressful. When you need a time-out, transfer your chosen words to strips of paper and toss them in your worry box or basket to house for a while.

Create a vision board of promising possibilities to shift your attention away from dwelling on uncertainty and negative outcomes. Make a list here of various activities, experiences, words, goals, ideas, and values that inspire you. Find images to match these that you can cut out, then paste them on a poster board. Hang your vision board in a spot you can look at frequently as a reminder.

Attention to self-care is vital for staying grounded. Take time to include something each day, no matter how small. "Tend and befriend" goes a long way.

Make a list of your favorite self-care activities. Add any activities that you've been curious about but are not yet something you do.

Choose one activity from your list on the opposite page and make time for this today. How did you feel afterwards?

Select another self-care activity, one you can easily incorporate in your life each day for one week. Give an account of the outcome.

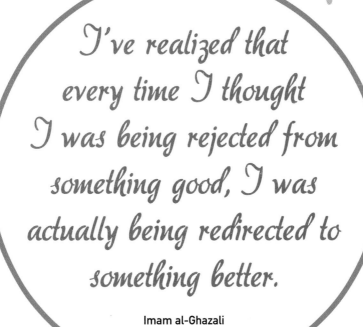

I've realized that
every time I thought
I was being rejected from
something good, I was
actually being redirected to
something better.

Imam al-Ghazali

Reframing from the negative to the positive in how you see, think, or speak about a situation will help you feel more centered and motivated to make a change. Sometimes you just need to shake up what feels stagnant to shift direction and get inspired.

Embrace the power of reframing and write down as many positive words that come to mind beginning with "re"/"re-".

_____

_____

_____

_____

_____

_____

_____

_____

Write a sentence or two reframing a current challenge using some of the words listed above.

_____

_____

_____

_____

_____

_____

_____

_____

_____

In your personal life and in the lives of others, how do you stand your ground and what do you stand up for?

Envision yourself in the future—in a particular situation in your life or the overall picture. Imagine how well all is going for you and describe the details.

Belonging and surrounding yourself with a supportive network is important for a sense of stability.

Who are the people you can be your authentic self around? Which organizations are closely aligned with your core values?

_____

_____

_____

_____

_____

_____

_____

_____

_____

Strengthen your bond with others and convey your gratitude. Choose one person or organization from the list above and contact them this week with a letter, email, text, call, or even voice memo to share a message of thanks for their support. Describe the experience and outcome.

_____

_____

_____

_____

_____

_____

_____

_____

The uplift of joy and laughter is just as contagious as the grip of fear and worry. It is important to find space for lightening up, even in the face of adversity.

List three things, or people, that always make you laugh.

1 _____

_____

2 _____

_____

3 _____

_____

Write about your most joyful memory.

_____

_____

_____

_____

_____

_____

_____

_____

_____

_____

_____

_____

_____

Create a personal list of your top ten reasons to stay grounded for today and in the future.

do something today
that your future self
will thank you for.

do something today
that your future self
will thank you for.